WS

Kathryn Heling and Deborah Hembrook

Clothesline Clues to Jobs People Do

Illustrated by Andy Robert Davies

🖼 Charlesbridge

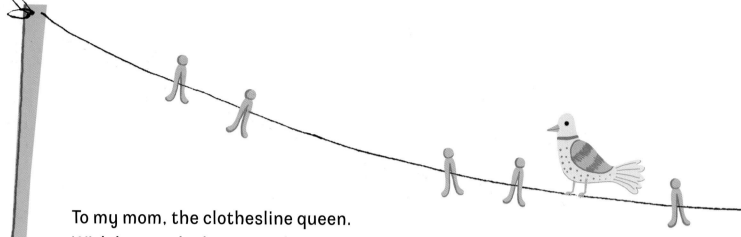

To my mom, the clothesline queen.
With love and admiration from your firstborn.–K. H.

To my mom, who encouraged me to pursue the job
I was meant to do. All my love.–D. H.

For Samantha.–A. R. D.

First paperback editon 2014
Text copyright © 2012 by Kathryn Heling and Deborah Hembrook
Illustrations copyright © 2012 by Andy Robert Davies

Published by Charlesbridge
85 Main Street
Watertown, MA 02472
(617) 926-0329
www.charlesbridge.com

Library of Congress Cataloging-in-Publication Data
Heling, Kathryn.
    Clothesline clues to jobs people do / Kathryn Heling
and Deborah Hembrook: Illustrated by Andy Robert
Davies.
        p. cm.
    ISBN 978-1-58089-251-3 (reinforced for library use)
    ISBN 978-1-58089-252-0 (softcover)
    ISBN 978-1-60734-447-6 (ebook pdf)
1. Vocational guidance–Juvenile literature. 2.
Occupations–Juvenile literature. 3. Professions–
Juvenile literature. I. Hembrook, Deborah. II. Davies, Andy
Robert. III. Title.
HF5381.2.H45 2012
331.702–dc23   2011025700

Printed in Singapore
(hc) 10 9 8 7 6 5 4
(sc) 10 9 8 7 6 5 4 3

Illustrations done in pencil and mixed media,
    manipulated digitally
Display type and text type set in Jesterday
Color separations by KHL Chroma Graphics, Singapore
Printed by Imago in Singapore
    Production supervision by Brian G. Walker
Designed by Susan Mallory Sherman and
    Whitney Leader-Picone

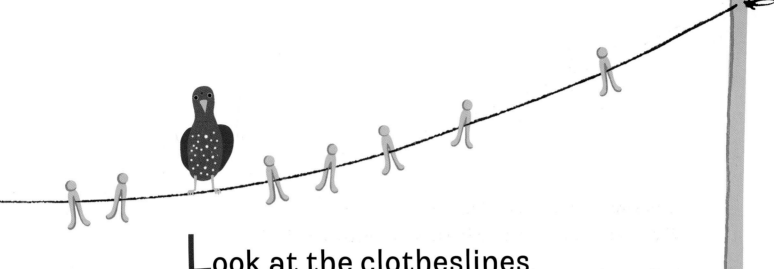

Look at the clotheslines
and see every clue!
Who uses these things
for the jobs that they do?

Uniform and cap,
an invite for you.
Big bag of letters.
What job does she do?

She is a mail carrier.

Milk pail and straw hat,
overalls in blue.
Plaid shirt, bandanna.
What job does he do?

He is a farmer.

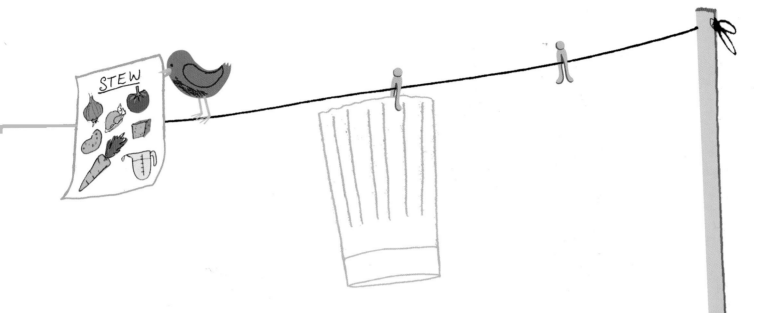

Oven mitts, apron,
recipe for stew.
Puffy hat and whisk.
What job does he do?

He is a chef.

Smock, beret, and brushes,
paints of every hue.
Canvas and easel.
What job does he do?

He is an artist.

Coveralls, tool belt,
work gloves and glue.
Safety glasses, saw.
What job does she do?

She is a carpenter.

Heavy pants, helmet,
wide suspenders, too.
Rescue coat, long hose.
What job does she do?

She is a firefighter.

Space suit and jet pack,
star charts to review.
Flight gloves and moon boots.
What job does she do?

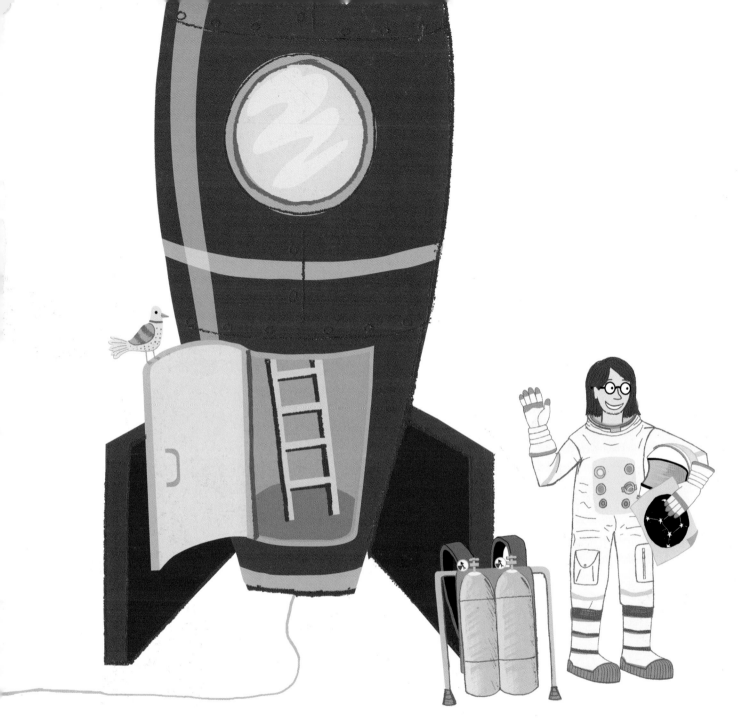

She is an astronaut.

These clothes are all clues
to jobs people do.
Is one of these jobs
just right for you?